Preventing car theft and crime in car parks

Crime prevention series
General Editor, Paul R. Wilson

Preventing car theft and crime in car parks

Susan Geason and Paul R. Wilson

Australian Institute of Criminology

First published 1990 by Australian Institute of Criminology, Canberra

© Australian Institute of Criminology

National Library of Australia
Cataloguing-in-publication entry

Geason, Susan, 1946-
    Preventing car theft and crime in car parks.

    Bibliography.
    ISBN 0 642 14939 9.

    1. Automobile theft — Australia. 2. Automobile theft - Australia — Prevention. 3. Crime prevention — Australia. I.Wilson, Paul R. (Paul Richard), 1941- . II. Australian Institute of Criminology. III. Title.   (Series : Crime prevention series).

364.1620994

Typeset by Renwick Pride, Albury, NSW
Printed and bound by Union Offset Co. Pty Ltd, Canberra

Designed by Adrian Young *MCSD*

Foreword

Car theft is a major problem in Australia as the following statistics show. In 1987–1988, 120,305 vehicles were stolen Australia wide, and in 1988–89 this increased to 122,542. A large number of these vehicles were never recovered which would indicate that car theft has become a serious organised criminal activity.

A number of preventive measures have been suggested. In particular, vehicle identification number (VIN) labelling has been proposed for vehicle components. Component labelling would undoubtedly have an effect on the trade in stolen spare parts. In addition, a new central Vehicle Identification Number computer register came into existence on 1 January 1989, which in time will enable registration authorities throughout Australia to make checks when processing applications for original registration, or processing applications for interstate transfer of registrations.

However, there is still much to be done. *Preventing Car Theft and Crime in Car Parks* suggests simple preventive measures for motor vehicle owners; offers practical advice to car manufacturers on improving car security features; and describes environmental design strategies useful for local authorities.

Duncan Chappell
Director

Contents

List of Tables

List of Figures

Introduction

The Australian Insurance Council (February 1989) estimates that, in the last ten financial years — 1978–79 to 1987–88 — 954,547 motor vehicles, valued at $4.7 billion, have been stolen Australia-wide (based on an average estimate of today's value at $5,000 per motor vehicle).

It is estimated that a car is stolen in Australia every six minutes. According to police statistics, about 12 per cent of cars stolen were left unlocked, and about 8 per cent had keys left in the ignition. Tables 1 and 2 reveal the severity of this problem.

Table 1 *Number and Value of Vehicles Stolen by State 1986–87 to 1987–88*

State	No. of Motor Vehicles Stolen 1986–87	Amount $*	No. of Motor Vehicles Stolen 1987–88	Amount $*
Victoria	30,626	153,130,000	29,621	148,105,000
New South Wales	65,331	326,655,000	53,092	265,460,000
Queensland	10,196	50,980,000	10,008	50,040,000
Australian Capital Territory	1,137	5,685,000	1,411	7,055,000
Western Australia	13,012	65,060,000	13,247	66,235,000
South Australia	10,118	50,590,000	10,166	50,830,000
Tasmania	982	4,910,000	1,223	6,115,000
Northern Territory	1,273	6,365,000	1,198	5,990,000
TOTALS	132,675	663,375,000	119,966	599,830,000

*Based on average estimate at today's [1989] value of $5,000 per motor vehicle.

Source: *ICA Bulletin*, February 1989, p. 7.

Table 2 *Number of Vehicles Stolen and Value 1978–79 to 1987–88*

Year	No. of Motor Vehicles Stolen	Amount $*
1987–88	119,966	599,830,000
1986–87	132,675	663,375,000
1985–86	118,607	593,035,000
1984–85	102,868	514,340,000
1983–84	96,317	481,585,000
1982–83	94,776	473,880,000
1981–82	80,353	401,765,000
1980–81	70,696	353,480,000
1979–80	70,551	352,755,000
1978–79	67,738	338,690,000
TOTAL	954,547	4,772,735,000

*Based on average estimate at today's [1989] value of $5,000 per motor vehicle.

Source: *ICA Bulletin*, February 1989, p. 7.

Just as the risk of car theft is high, the likelihood that the thief will be apprehended and the vehicle recovered is low. According to 1987–88 New South Wales Police Department (1988) statistics, of the 64,700 car thefts recorded in New South Wales, only 1,776 — or 2.74 per cent — were cleared up. The clear-up rate in country areas was higher, at 9.26 per cent, but even lower — 1.86 per cent — in the Sydney metropolitan area.

Clearly, a concerted effort is needed to reduce car theft and theft from cars and to make stolen cars and car parts identifiable.

The approach

This study combines a situational approach to the prevention of car crime with longer-term educational strategies.

Situational crime prevention strategies are directed at changing the environment to prevent a crime from happening, rather than attempting to change the behaviour of the offender or to ameliorate the social conditions — unemployment, alienation, inadequate social conditioning etc. — which might have given rise to the crime in the first place.

Situational crime prevention is also referred to as opportunity reduction, that is, making it harder for the offender to commit a crime; in this case making it harder to take or steal from a car or to commit acts of violence in car parks. Situational strategies include controlling access to and improving surveillance of car parks, and target hardening through improving the design of cars to make them more difficult to break into and start. (For more information on the theoretical aspects of situational crime prevention, see *Crime prevention: theory and practice*, by Susan Geason and Paul Wilson, Australian Institute of Criminology, Canberra, 1988.)

We also look at a number of educational programs — to teach drivers to take more responsibility for the safety of their own vehicles, to raise drivers' consciousness on the need for better safety equipment in cars, and to encourage manufacturers to improve the security features of their vehicles.

The problem

Australia

Autocrime takes two forms: theft *from* cars and theft *of* cars. Large public car parks pose other threats as well: poor lighting and lack of surveillance can turn them into hangouts for vandals, robbers and rapists.

In 1986–87, 132,675 motor vehicles were stolen in Australia, costing insurance companies an estimated $53.7 million (Insurance Council of Australia 1988). Since 1978, thieves have made off with 834,581 vehicles, at an estimated cost of $3.3 billion. According to the Insurance Council, 12,000 of those vehicles were left unlocked, and owners left keys in the ignition of 6,500 of them, indicating that simple common sense precautions could have prevented 18,500 car thefts and saved an estimated $74 million.

About 27 per cent of cars were stolen from car parks and over a third from near owners' homes. In fact, 25 per cent of the latter were stolen outside the owner's home and nearly 9 per cent from the owner's driveway, while 20 per cent were stolen from other streets (*Weekend Australian* 28–29 May 1988). A 1987 New South Wales Police Task Force maintained that 69 per cent of the State's car thieves arrested were 18 or younger.

Although New South Wales still has the highest theft rate in Australia, this has fallen more steeply than other States, and is at its lowest level since 1981. The incidence of theft also fell in Victoria, the Australian Capital Territory and Western Australia; South Australia's remained stationary and Tasmania's increased.

New South Wales

In the 1987–88 financial year, 56,000 cars were stolen in New South Wales, and the National Roads and Motorists Association (NRMA May 1989) estimated the direct cost to the community of theft of cars in 1988 as $113 million. The police estimate that each year they devote 100,000 hours to recording car theft crime statistics before any investigation is undertaken. Auto theft is therefore one of the most costly crimes in terms of police resources when both time and manpower are considered.

Theft of cars has been decreasing, however, with 1987–88 numbers down 18 per cent and costs down $9 million over 1986–87. The NRMA speculates that increased public awareness and police activity are responsible for the drop in car thefts.

Sydney — car theft capital of the world?

Car theft in Australia is worst in metropolitan Sydney, with the Chief Insurance Executive of the NRMA calling it 'the car theft capital of the world' (*Sydney Morning Herald* 3 June 1988). He said Friday was the worst time for car theft, and Sunday the lowest risk day. Most car thefts took place between 6 pm and 6 am and the street was the worst place to park.

The pattern of car thefts in metropolitan Sydney is changing, however. In 1987 there were 25 suburbs (or postcode areas) which were classified as extreme or high theft risk areas, compared to 41 in 1986. In 1988 this dropped to 20.

In 1988 Liverpool took over from Cabramatta as the worst area for theft of cars. In 1988, as in the previous year, Sydney City was the worst area for theft from cars, with 1988 claim numbers running four times higher than those from Cabramatta, the second worst area.

The thieves

The NRMA divides car thieves into four key groups — professionals, joyriders, petty thieves and fraudulent claimants. In 1987–88:

• professionals accounted for 38 per cent of car thefts or 54 per cent of the total cost of car theft;

• joyriders stole about 36 per cent of cars at 23 per cent of the total cost;

• petty thieves were responsible for almost 22 per cent of the number and 16 per cent of the cost; and

• fraud, running at a little over 4 per cent, accounted for over 7 per cent of the cost (NRMA May 1988).

The proportion of insurance claims arising from fraud and petty theft has fallen from its 1987 level, but the incidence of professional theft grew — up from 24 to 39 per cent. Professional theft remains the most costly element of theft claims.

Target vehicles

Older models are the main target for theft, while new cars are the major targets of accessory stripping. Luxury vehicles and sports cars are the highest-risk cars to own. Sports cars are the most popular type of car stolen, particularly by professionals, while late-model luxury vehicles show the highest incidence of 'theft from' claims — for example: Audi, Mercedes Benz, Peugeot, Statesman, Range Rover and a large number of Ford models.

Vehicle theft is most widespread in older vehicles, particularly those manufactured before 1980. Early model Belmont/Kingswoods, Commodores, Statesmans, Sunbirds, Cortinas, Escorts and Celicas fared poorly, though later models of these makes improved. Late models with high theft risk include the Fairlane, Fairmont Ghia, LTD, Statesman, and the Mitsubishi Lancer. The Bronco is the most stolen off-road vehicle.

High-quality stereo systems are still the most popular items stolen from cars. BMW have fought back by installing stereos that require a Personal Identification Number (PIN) for activation with the result that the 'theft from' claim frequency for late model BMWs dropped from 48 per thousand to 10 between 1986 and 1988.

Target locations

In Sydney cars parked on streets are the main target for thieves, accounting for 50 per cent of stolen cars, with public car parks next at 15 per cent — down from 23 per cent (NRMA May 1989). The number of thefts from shopping centres remained stable at 9.5 per cent. There has also been an increase in the number of cars stolen from club car parks and off-street parking (see Table 3).

These statistics correspond with those in a 1982 British crime survey showing that 23 per cent of stolen cars had been parked in the street, while only 14 per cent were stolen from a driveway and 6 per cent from a garage (Clarke May 1987). The message for car owners is obvious — if you have a garage or driveway, use it. The message for town planners is also clear — providing garage space or off-street parking can help reduce car theft.

Thursdays, Fridays and Saturdays are the most active days for car theft, and Sundays the quietest. The majority of car thefts — 55 per cent — occur at night.

Table 3 *Where Cars are Stolen in Sydney, NSW, 1988*

	Overall	In High-risk Areas
Street	47.9%	10.5%
Car park (other)	14.9%	30.7%
Off Street	13.3%	9.6%
Shopping Centre	9.5%	22.0%
Railway	5.8%	17.3%
Club	5.7%	13.4%
Other	2.8%	9.2%

Source: NRMA 1989, *Car Theft in New South Wales.*

The solutions

The first step in analysing the scope for preventing car theft is an understanding of the factors contributing to the scale of the problem. Any list of such factors would have to include:

- the pool of potential offenders

- the number of cars on the road

- the 'demand' for stolen cars (either for temporary use or for retention)

- the 'costs' of car theft in terms of risk and consequences of detection, and

- the ease or difficulty of car theft in terms of security.

After analysing these factors, Ronald Clarke (1987) concluded that the most profitable course of action would be to make car theft more difficult. He came up with five main ways of doing this:

- encouraging better security habits among car owners

- designing and constructing more secure cars

- improving vehicle identification and registration procedures — perhaps adopting the United States VIN or Vehicle Identification Number system, for example

- tightening insurance practices

- regulating the smash repair/rebuilding trade.

Professor Clarke concentrated on the first two options as these have been the subject of most research and discussion. As this publication is concerned with the safety and security of car parks as well as preventing theft of cars, we have added some crime prevention through environmental design (CPTED) strategies.

Encouraging better security habits

Educating the public

Although a public education campaign at Airport West Shopping

Town (see following study) seems to have worked, there is some evidence that we may be close to the optimum level of compliance on exhortations to lock cars; that is, we can go on talking, but no more people are going to take notice.

And as Ron Clarke pointed out in his paper to the NRMA's Putting on the Brakes seminar in May 1987, a United Kingdom Home Office evaluation of two public education campaigns — a national campaign involving TV and national newspaper advertising, and a local police-directed campaign relying on distribution of leaflets and free publicity from local media — showed that neither campaign had a demonstrable effect on the number of reported thefts or the proportion of cars found secure in spot checks by the police.

Case study: Airport West Shopping Town, Victoria

A pilot program run by Victorian police has shown that simple precautions such as locking cars and taking keys with you can reduce car theft from car parks in major shopping towns. During the program, car thefts remained stable at Airport West Shopping Town but rose throughout the rest of Victoria.

Between November 1987 and January 1988, Broadmeadows Police's Community Involvement Program and Westfield Limited ran a public education program at the shopping town exhorting the public to:

- lock their cars
- make sure they had their keys with them, and
- put valuables in cars out of sight.

Signs containing these messages were erected in the car park; inside the shopping centres posters were displayed and a 30-second tape was played repeatedly over the public address system.

Westfield Limited has decided to extend the program to all its Victorian shopping towns, and Broadmeadows Police's Community Involvement Program found the results sufficiently encouraging to repeat the program over the July-September period, when car thefts are traditionally high.

It has been suggested that the police check statistics for theft from cars during the pilot program, as this could well have been a positive spin-off from the car theft prevention program.

According to Ron Clarke, who spoke at the NRMA's 1987 seminar on car theft, the NRMA's approach (*see* case study below) was more effective.

Case study: NRMA campaign

In May 1987, the NRMA launched its 'Make Life Hell for Car Thieves' public education campaign, directed primarily at reducing easy opportunities for car theft.

Car security surveys had shown them that one in five parked vehicles was left unsecured, with either a door unlocked or a window open or both. As well, 25 per cent of car owners who had car alarms had not switched them on before their car was stolen.

The NRMA's campaign focused on raising the individual's awareness of the risk of car theft. People were given detailed information about the risks they ran depending on where they lived, where they parked their cars and what kinds of vehicles thieves preferred.

The television launch of the campaign was carried out at Westfield Shopping Complex at Parramatta, Sydney's worst location for stolen vehicles. (A spin-off from this decision was that Westfield has improved security at the complex, and the theft rate has declined sharply since that time.) The following day a seminar, 'Car Theft — Putting on the Brakes', jointly organised by the Australian Institute of Criminology and the NRMA, was held.

A package of brochures was distributed through NRMA branches, with 100,000 given out on request in the first eight weeks and another 100,000 reprinted. Community service messages were screened; half-page advertisements were placed in regional newspapers; shopping centre displays were mounted; advertisements were run in selected movie theatres to reach young people; and the Association's magazine, *The Open Road*, which has a readership of 1.5 million, ran editorials and features to reinforce the message of the campaign.

In addition, the NRMA held discussions with Neighbourhood Watch groups (which it sponsors in New South Wales and the Australian Capital Territory) to concentrate awareness at the local level and focus on 'hotspots' for car theft in particular areas, usually centering on the commercial and shopping districts.

It is not yet clear whether the campaign was successful in changing individuals' attitudes, though the organisers saw a connection between the campaign and the fact that 20 per cent of car alarms and ignition fuel cut-off switches fitted to vehicles in the research sample had been fitted after the campaign started.

The impact of the campaign on car theft seems somewhat ambiguous, as a significant decline in these offences occurred just before the campaign started. Research did, however, show a further 19 per cent decline in car thefts after the 'Make Life Hell for Thieves' campaign was run. Follow-up research could be needed to ascertain the long-term effects of the campaign.

Educating car manufacturers

Case study: the NRMA car stealability ratings

In 1989 the NRMA evaluated ten locally-made and three imported cars to test how easily they could be stolen (*The Open Road* February 1989). The Car Security Evaluation was carried out by the Assessing Division of NRMA Insurance with the assistance of the organisation's Technical Department and Road Service, and rated the cars on a stealability scale ranging from a low of 0 to a high of 100 points for security features (*see* Table 4).

Local vehicles used in the evaluation were Ford Falcon EA, Ford Laser KE, Ford Telstar AT, Mitsubishi Magna TN, Toyota Camry, Toyota Corolla, Holden Commodore VN, Holden Camira JE, Nissan Skyline and the Nissan Pulsar. The imported models were the Volvo 740 GL, the Mercedes-Benz 300E and the BMW 320i, none of which are regarded as luxury vehicles in their home markets.

Car security was evaluated on ease of entry and starting, with 35 points awarded for entry features, 30 for features of the ignition lock, and 35 points for other security aspects such as security alarms and coded access to ignition and stereo systems. A score of over 50 was considered acceptable, based on the highest-equipped standard vehicle known in terms of security — the BMW 735i, which scored 90 points out of 100.

The BMW 735i has the following standard security features:

•   central locking deadlock system activated by an infra-red remote system and a central locking, multi-position switch;

•   special one-sided anti-theft ignition and door key;

•   anti-theft radio activated by coded number once ignition is turned off; and

• a horizontal position switch — motor switch — activating the car alarm.

The Ford Laser KE/Mazda came in with the lowest score, rating only five points, and the two top locally-made cars — the Nissan Skyline and the Commodore VN — scored below the acceptable level of 50+ points. Of the three imported models, one scored over 50 (Volvo 740) and two scored over 60 (Mercedes 300E and BMW 320i).

Table 4 *Car Security Rating Points Table*
[Higher points mean better security rating]

Car	Entry (0-35)	Ignition (0-30)	Other (0-35)	Total (0-100)
Ford Laser KE	3	2	0	5
Holden Camira JE	3	7	0	10
Ford Telstar AT	10	2	0	12
Toyota Corolla	12	2	9	14
Honda Prelude	12	2	0	14
Ford Falcon EA	17	3	0	20
Mitsubishi Magna TN*	14	6	0	20
Toyota Camry	12	12	0	24
Nissan Pulsar	11	23	0	34
Holden Commodore VN	27	15	0	42
Nissan Skyline	17	23	0	40
Volvo 740	28	23	0	51
Mercedes 300E	27	28	5	60
BMW 320i	35	18	10	63

*Following modifications made to the door locks of post-June 1988 Mitsubishi Magnas, the entry points have been revised from 14 to 21, giving a total score of 27.

Source: NRMA. *The Open Road*, February 1989.

A spokesman for the NRMA pointed out that for cars which are popular with thieves — for example the Ford Laser and the Ford Falcon — entry took less than ten seconds and starting the car took between ten and 20 seconds. He said the types of locks used for ignition and doors on most of the cars were vastly inferior to all but the most rudimentary household locks.

Though locally-produced cars fared badly in the evaluation, the NRMA pointed out that, if the good features exhibited by these cars were combined in one vehicle, its theft resistance would be quite high. These good features were:

• the Commodore door lock and handle

- the inner door shielding on the Falcon
- the door button from the Skyline
- lock mechanism on the Corolla and Camry
- ignition lock from Skyline or Pulsar, and
- ignition lock position of Magna or Camira.

If a clearly identified coded stereo system, preferably with a flashing light, were added, the composite car's security rating would be very high.

The NRMA has submitted its findings to the manufacturers of the vehicles tested in the survey. It has also made a video demonstrating to manufacturers just how easily their vehicles can be penetrated by thieves and is hopeful that manufacturers will respond by adding safety features to popular models of cars.

If what manufacturers say is true — that security does not sell cars — there is obviously a need to raise public consciousness on this subject. The NRMA is endeavouring to do so by circulating the security ratings to its two million members through its magazine *The Open Road*.

The magazine article on car security was accompanied by an advertisement for *How to Protect Your Car*, an NRMA booklet on car theft. This is available at all NRMA branch offices, district depots and at Head Office, 151 Clarence Street, Sydney, 2000.

Design solutions

For its part, the car industry could become more involved in the fate of its vehicles once they leave the showroom.

Clarke (1987) believes the industry has a public duty to provide secure cars, just as it does to provide safe, non-polluting and energy-efficient ones. He takes this line because the costs of insecure cars are not borne just by the victims of car theft, but by everybody, by way of increased insurance premiums and police and court time.

He points out that the United States Government introduced legislation in 1984 compelling manufacturers to improve the security of their most vulnerable models.

Clarke also sees designing in improved security, or designing out vulnerability as a more useful long-term strategy than trying to change people's habits.

Though a substantial proportion of all vehicle crimes are committed by determined professional thieves, Clarke argues most are
undertaken by casual thieves making the most of the opportunities
provided by vehicle design. Opportunities for crime can be minimised
by producing more secure vehicles, thus increasing the risk the thief
has to take. A much more secure vehicle can be produced at little if
any additional cost, using available components and technology.

Three examples will demonstrate the potential of vehicle design to
reduce autocrime:

•   In 1970 the steering column lock was introduced as a standard
feature on all cars manufactured or imported into the United Kingdom. Home Office investigations in the mid-70s found that cars without steering column locks were three times more likely to be stolen
than those with them (United Kingdom Home Office 1985).

•   Similarly, car thefts dropped by 60 per cent after steering column
locks were made compulsory on all vehicles in West Germany in 1963
(Mayhew et al. 1976). There is a need for effective steering column
locks in new cars in Australia in both less expensive and luxury cars
particularly given the NRMA's claim that Sydney is 'the car theft capital of the world'.

•   In the United States a study by General Motors found that cars fitted with alarm systems as standard equipment were 20 per cent less
likely to be stolen than equivalent cars without alarms (Clarke 1987).
Car thieves are highly ingenious, however, and increased cooperation
between car manufacturers and police will be necessary to beat them
at their own game.

British research

In consultation with car and vehicle component manufacturers, the
police and car users, Southall and Ekblom (1985) on behalf of the
United Kingdom Home Office developed a number of criteria for
assessing car security measures, viz. cost, convenience and reliability,
safety, design freedom and cost effectiveness.

Their group discussions with drivers in the United Kingdom indi-
cated that, if properly informed about the risks of autocrime and the
scope for reducing it through design, people would be prepared to
pay more — perhaps as much as £50 ($100) extra — for a car.
Besides, if car manufacturers began to compete on security, the cost

would be less important. As well, mass production should lower prices.

The authors also pointed out that effective security required design of the security of the car as a whole, and advised designers to adopt a wide range of approaches to particular security functions if they wanted to stay a step ahead of the thieves. Finally, Southall and Ekblom recommended a staged approach to improving car security.

Research carried out for the United Kingdom Home Office by the Institute for Consumer Ergonomics at Loughborough University has shown that car security can be greatly improved with minimal interference to the design of cars, at relatively little cost and in a manner which imposes no inconvenience to the motorist.

Building on the clear but limited gains from such crime prevention measures as the steering column lock, *Southall and Ekblom (1985), Designing for Car Security: towards a crime free car*, argued that a significant and progressive reduction in car crime could be achieved within the next decade.

The report made the case for designed-in car security. It argued that technology was available with the potential to lead to significant reductions in vulnerability, and that a long-term investment in microelectronic technology would pay off for motor manufacturers.

The Home Office study concluded that the production of a car immune from most opportunistic theft required no major redesign of existing vehicles or the addition of any expensive devices; and that there need be no inconvenience to users, no special problems with reliability, and no compromise on safety.

It maintained that, while simple mechanical solutions may currently be the best approach for low value cars, it should be possible to develop more sophisticated electrical or electronic solutions for more expensive cars. Many mechanical solutions are already available and require minimal development; although many prototype electronic security devices exist, their application needs more research and development, however.

The study predicted that, if design efforts began immediately, even the least expensive base models could, in five years time, be made far less vulnerable to theft of the car or its contents.

The crime-proof car

According to the report, a typical car could have the following standard, factory-fitted security package:

- securely installed high security locks on all doors and boot

- no protruding sill buttons

- a high-security, well installed steering column lock

- laminated (or equivalent) side and rear window glass

- protected bonnet release catches

- shielded internal door latching components

- an audible reminder to remove keys from ignition

- catches of tipping seats housed in the boot and not in the passenger compartment

- the boot well of hatchbacks protected by a steel cover incorporating a lock, providing a secure place to leave valuables.

More expensive models might also include:

- alarms

- central locking

- mobilisation of the engine through its electronic management system.

The authors predicted that, while mechanical features might still be the first line of defence in ten years time, electrical and electronic features should be more widely available. Electrical locking systems could also replace mechanical locks on base models, which might also be fitted with alarms and electronic engine immobilisation.

If multiplexing is more widespread, this microprocessor-based system could significantly increase the sophistication of electronic engine immobilisation, alarms and door locking devices. Multiplexing is a method of reducing the number of wiring circuits in the car by transmitting coded signals along single wires. Cars with multiplexing would carry a number of microprocessors, making the equipment for interpreting entry codes available for use at little additional cost.

As electronic systems facilitating immobilisation, storage of vehicle identification information and access to cars will only respond to electronic codes, tampering will require a much higher degree of skill on the part of thieves than simply cutting wires.

Figure 1 *The Crime-proof Car*

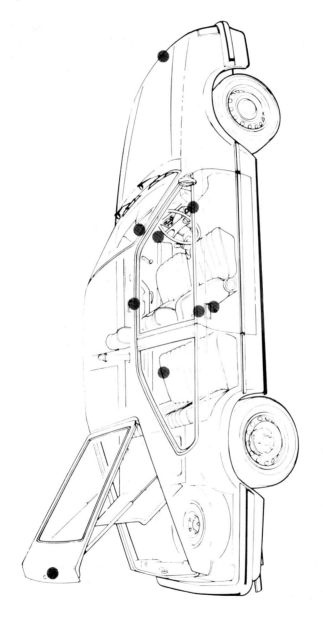

Source: United Kingdom Home Office 1985, *Design Solutions to Autocrime*. Reproduced with the permission of the Controller of Her Majesty's Stationery Office, London.

Case study: the Rover security concepts car

Rover addressed three major requirements in its Sterling 800 secure car — preventing the thief from entering, making the car protest if its defences were breached, and preventing the protesting car from being driven away (*Austin Rover News* 6 December 1988).

Their design solutions centred on locking and door systems, alarms, glazing and in-car entertainment.

Locks

• The vehicle has no external door locks, rather a superlocking system activated by an infra-red transmitter.

• All door latches are fully enclosed to prevent manipulation.

• Removing the ignition key inhibits the electronic engine management system and immobilises the car.

• Audible warnings are fitted to remind the driver that s/he has not removed the key, locked the car or set the alarm.

Alarm and glazing

• The alarm system is triggered by doors, bonnet and boot and also includes an ultra-sonic sensor to detect movement within the vehicle.

• A continuity strip is fitted to the glazing on one side of the car: this triggers the alarm if the glass is broken. While the alarm is activated the ignition system is totally immobilised.

• On the other side of the car, the alternative of laminated glass is fitted in specially-strengthened door frames, and all fixed glasses are bonded to the bodywork to prevent easy removal.

• Should the vehicle's electrical system fail for any reason, access is effected via a non-pick boot lock which is enclosed in a steel cage to resist attack. Inside the boot a back-up battery can be activated with the same key to unlock the vehicle.

• Wheel rotation sensors are fitted to detect movement if an attempt is made to tow the car away, and another sensor detects jacking if someone attempts to remove a wheel. Locking wheel nuts are an added deterrent.

Figure 2 *The Rover Sterling 800 security concepts car*

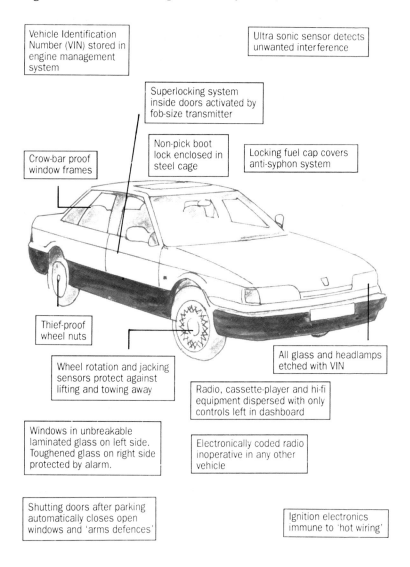

Vehicle Identification Number (VIN) stored in engine management system

Ultra sonic sensor detects unwanted interference

Superlocking system inside doors activated by fob-size transmitter

Non-pick boot lock enclosed in steel cage

Crow-bar proof window frames

Locking fuel cap covers anti-syphon system

Thief-proof wheel nuts

Wheel rotation and jacking sensors protect against lifting and towing away

All glass and headlamps etched with VIN

Radio, cassette-player and hi-fi equipment dispersed with only controls left in dashboard

Windows in unbreakable laminated glass on left side. Toughened glass on right side protected by alarm.

Electronically coded radio inoperative in any other vehicle

Shutting doors after parking automatically closes open windows and 'arms defences'

Ignition electronics immune to 'hot wiring'

Source: *Daily Mail* (London) 7 December 1988. Reproduced by permission.

In-Car Entertainment

• The in-car entertainment system is split into a number of modular units spaced around the interior of the car.

• All controls are housed in the instrument binnacle and styled to suit the Rover 800.

• The cassette player and controls are in the conventional position with the system amplifier housed behind the fascia.

• Security coding, already a feature of Austin Rover sets, is also fitted, making the whole system thief proof.

Vehicle Identification

• The Vehicle Identification Number (VIN) has been added to a plate in the windscreen area, and all major components are identified by the same number using tamper-proof labels which are destroyed on removal.

• This same VIN number is stored within the electronic engine management system and can be read at any service.

• All glazing and headlamps carry the VIN and car registration number. Petrol thieves are foiled by an anti-syphon fuel filler and lockable petrol cap.

Independent Assessment

The effectiveness of the Rover Sterling 800 has been tested by a team of police and an independent car crime consultant. They could find no way of opening the doors, boot or bonnet by non-destructive means. And even with the windows smashed, the superlocked doors could not be opened, because the sill buttons remained inoperable.

For cost reasons, Austin Rover is not predicting that the sophisticated systems engineered into this model will be applied as factory fitted items down to small cars such as the Metro. They do think it possible, however, that individual items could be available, either as standard, options or accessories within the Austin Rover range in the future.

The following section looks at the design problems associated with building a crime-proof car and examines existing and in-development solutions — from mechanical solutions to the latest in electrical and electronic devices and systems.

Mechanical solutions

Locks: The disc tumbler lock fitted to the doors, boot or tailgate of most cars suffers from a number of weaknesses. Many locks become more vulnerable as they begin to wear through regular use. If a lock is to be effective, it should not be possible to operate with any device other than the proper key, even when the lock is jiggled or manipulated.

Locks also need to be stronger, that is, more resistant to force within the lock itself and in its mounting within the body panel.

Solutions: Some manufacturers have redesigned locks so they are stronger and do not become insecure through wear. Locks can be made more resistant to force by hardened steel plates within the lock and mounting the lock flush with the bodywork.

Case study: The Vauxhall Cavalier's deadlocks

Tests by *The Sunday Times* and the British Consumers' Association in October 1988 confirmed Vauxhall's claims that new locks fitted to the improved version of its Cavalier are the most secure yet produced.

A security expert failed to by-pass the locks after an eight-hour attempt. Of nearly 60 other models ranging from the Skoda Estelle to the Ford Sierra undergoing the same test, none survived. Some were defeated in three or four seconds, while the most secure took only 25 seconds to breach.

The key to the Vauxhall's impregnability is its deadlock system, which took two years and £1 million ($2 million) to develop. When the driver turns the door lock to the special anti-theft setting, a steel bolt drops into the lock housing, freezing the mechanisms. Attempts to slide steel wires or strips into the gap around the door frame are foiled by a series of bends. Even if the thief breaks a window, the doors cannot be unlocked from inside the car.

Figure 3 *New Lock Designs*

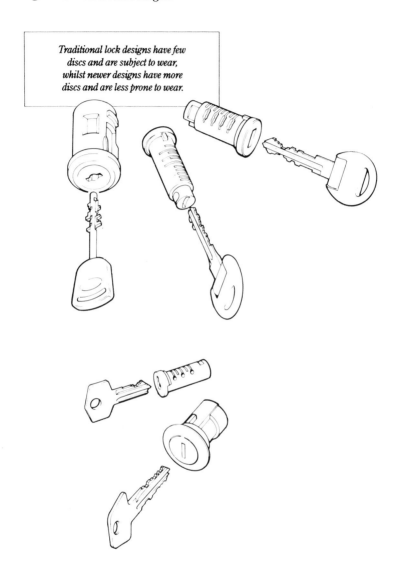

Traditional lock designs have few
discs and are subject to wear,
whilst newer designs have more
discs and are less prone to wear.

Source: United Kingdom Home Office 1985, *Design Solutions to
Autocrime*. Reproduced with the permission of the Controller of Her Majesty's Stationery Office, London.

Figure 4 The Vauxhall Cavalier's Locking System

'Thief proof' Vauxhall

(Section from above)

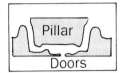

Labyrinth system: prevents lock being released with wire or steel strip

1 Special key setting activates dead lock

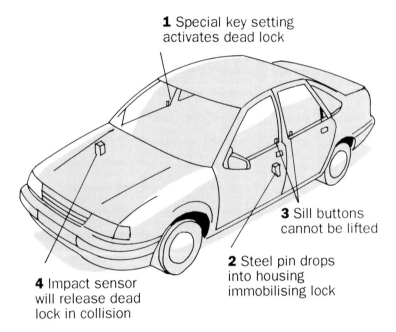

3 Sill buttons cannot be lifted

2 Steel pin drops into housing immobilising lock

4 Impact sensor will release dead lock in collision

Source: *Sunday Times* 9 October 1988. Reproduced by permission.

Door Latches: Mechanisms inside the door panel are vulnerable to tampering from outside the car.

Solutions: Simple shields within the door can protect latching arms and linkages, or carefully designed rods can prevent door latches being tampered with. Rods can be replaced by a Bowden cable (similar to a bicycle brake cable) routed in such a way that is inaccessible from outside the car. It is also important to ensure that holes in the exterior bodywork — those exposed when exterior trim is removed, for example — provide no access to these linkages. Protruding sill buttons should also be eliminated.

Windows: Some windows are made of toughened glass which shatters easily and gives access to the car or valuables inside.

Solutions: It is much more difficult to penetrate laminated glass than toughened glass. It may also be safer. This would help justify its higher cost, which may double or treble the cost of winding side windows. At the very least, laminated glass should be used for fixed quarter-lights which are easily broken to gain access to interior door handles.

In the future, other forms of glass or plastic may provide cheaper solutions.

Figure 5 *Secure Door Latches*

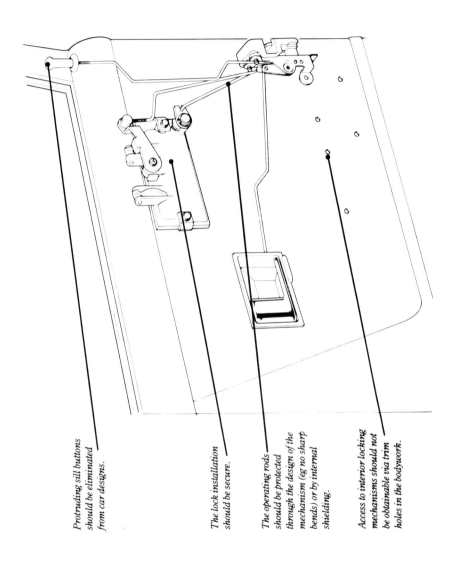

Protruding sill buttons should be eliminated from car designs.

The lock installation should be secure.

The operating rods should be protected through the design of the mechanism (eg no sharp bends) or by internal shielding.

Access to interior locking mechanisms should not be obtainable via trim holes in the bodywork.

Source: United Kingdom Home Office 1985, *Design Solutions to Autocrime.* Reproduced with the permission of the Controller of Her Majesty's Stationery Office, London.

Figure 6 *Secure Windows*

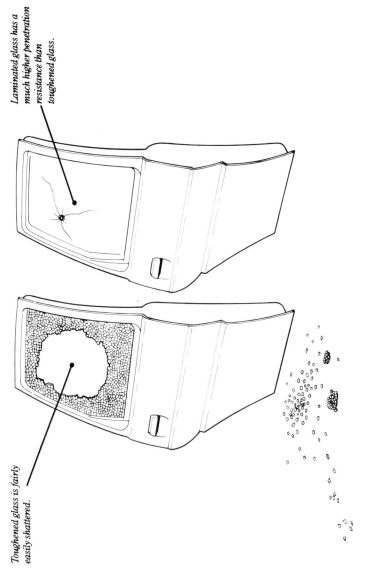

Laminated glass has a much higher penetration resistance than toughened glass.

Toughened glass is fairly easily shattered.

Source: United Kingdom Home Office 1985, *Design Solutions to Autocrime*. Reproduced with the permission of the Controller of Her Majesty's Stationery Office, London.

Vehicle immobilisation

Steering column locks: In the United Kingdom, United States, West Germany and other countries, regulations require the standard fit of a mechanical device for preventing the car being driven away. Although a few manufacturers have opted for transmission locking, the majority prefer the steering column lock. This is a very effective device in principle, but since its introduction, a number of design and installation weaknesses have been revealed.

Solutions: Both newer design high-security locks and secure installation methods are needed if the steering column lock is to work against thieves. For example, a rear-load lock — in which the lock barrel is inserted from the steering column end of the housing — is more secure than the front-load lock, which is assembled by inserting the barrel from the keyhole end.

Electrical and electronic security

With the growth in electrical and electronic systems in recent years, the potential exists to design in security devices such as alarm systems. In addition, electronics offers alternative, often more adaptable and effective, solutions to current mechanical vulnerabilities.

Door Security: Electrical locking has been available now for some years in the form of central locking systems. These are now an optional feature costing two to three times more than the mechanical locking system.

New systems have been developed, however. If fitted as standard on high volume production cars, these could add as little as 20 per cent to the cost of current mechanical locks

Electrical locks have the following advantages:

• Convenience and security; they ensure all other doors are locked when the driver's door is locked.

• If they wholly replace conventional systems, there are fewer mechanical components to be tampered with.

• Automatic door locking can be provided.

Figure 7 *Steering Column Lock*

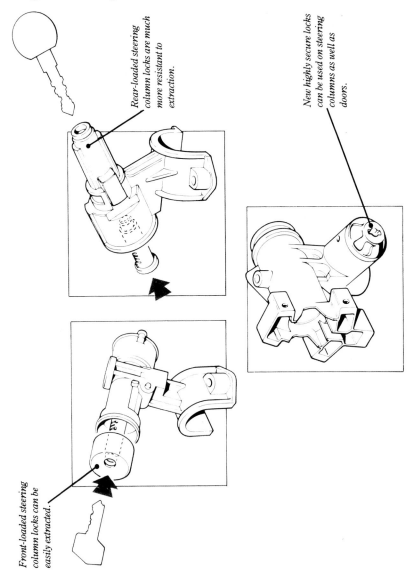

Rear-loaded steering column locks are much more resistant to extraction.

New highly secure locks can be used on steering columns as well as doors.

Front-loaded steering column locks can be easily extracted.

Source: United Kingdom Home Office 1985, *Design Solutions to Autocrime*. Reproduced with the permission of the Controller of Her Majesty's Stationery Office, London.

- While conventional metal keys will provide good security, electrical locking systems pave the way for new forms of high security key or access devices such as infra-red remote control units, keypads and magnetic cards.

Case study: electronic deadlocks on GM-H's Commodore

When it was Australia's top selling car in the early 1980s, the Commodore was also the top target for thieves. Representations from the NSW NRMA led GM-H to reinforce its door locks on the superseded VL Commodore and introduce improved systems, including the double-sided keys on their new VN model.

GM-H is now fitting an electronically-operated deadlock system as standard equipment in their top-line Commodore, the Calais, which retailed in 1989 for $31,265 and as an option on the $20,014 Executive and the mid-range $24,781 Berlina (*The Weekend Australian* December 3-4 1988). The Calais' standard equipment also includes an elaborate Italian-made Cobra alarm that activates a siren, the horn and turn indicators when it detects a forced entry through the doors, windows, bonnet and boot lid.

The deadlocks, similar to those in widespread household use, are triggered by a battery-powered, matchbox-sized sensor emitting UHF signals, and have a special anti-theft setting in which a high-tensile steel bolt drops into the lock housing and freezes the mechanism.

The system, which prevents all four doors being unlocked on the inside even if the windows are smashed, incorporates an impact sensor that automatically releases the locks in a collision. It was rated as impregnable by the British Consumers Association, which employed a security expert to test 60 cars using implements commonly used by thieves. The expert took only seven seconds to break into most cars, but failed to by-pass the electronic deadlocks after an eight-hour attempt.

GM-H says the system, perfected by its British counterpart, Vauxhall Motors at a cost of $2 million, will be available for all Holden models if there is sufficient demand.

Figure 8 *Electrical and Electronic Locking*

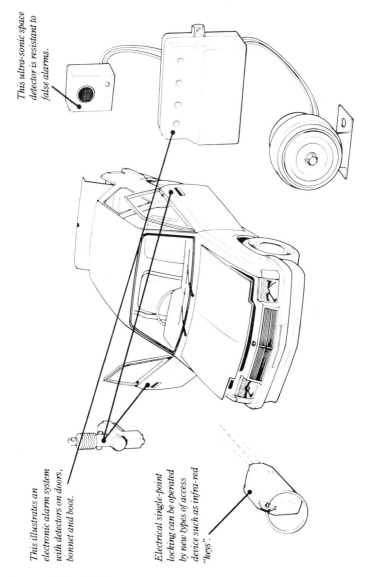

This ultra-sonic space detector is resistant to false alarms.

This illustrates an electronic alarm system with detectors on doors, bonnet and boot.

Electrical single-point locking can be operated by new types of access device such as infra-red "keys".

Source: United Kingdom Home Office 1985, *Design Solutions to Autocrime*. Reproduced with the permission of the Controller of Her Majesty's Stationery Office, London.

Alarm Systems: The problem with many existing alarm systems, particularly those installed by owners, is that they have a high rate of false alarms and are often easily disabled by thieves. New designs are less prone to false alarms, and having them fitted in the factory can ensure that the system is appropriate for the car and is properly installed.

Many sophisticated technologies offering greater protection through infra-red and ultra-sound are now available.

Some manufacturers offer an alarm system as a factory-fit option, while others offer a dealer-fit option. The cost of alarm systems could be halved if they were fitted as a standard on the production line rather than as an option.

Case study: Lojack radio-equipped car alarm

Available only in Massachusetts, in the United States, the Lojack radio-equipped car alarm makes it possible for police to locate stolen cars by picking up radio signals. In 1989 22,000 vehicles had the device.

The system is activated only after a theft is reported. Police enter the vehicle's identification number into the state police data bank and their computer sends a signal, using police radio towers, to the hidden receiver-transmitter in the stolen car. The signal causes the device to start broadcasting a code that can be picked up by police cruisers equipped with Lojack tracking computers in an area of about 25 to 50 square kilometres.

When the stolen car comes within range of a cruiser with a computer, a device in the cruiser beeps and displays the location of the stolen car, as well as a five-digit code. The police officer then types the code into the cruiser's computer and immediately receives a description of the stolen car, along with information about whether the theft occurred in conjunction with another crime. The police can then plan how to approach the vehicle.

According to the Massachusetts Governor's Auto Theft Strike Force, the system helped police find 754 vehicles — out of 789 that had Lojack when they were stolen — and make 104 arrests (*The New York Times* 2 September 1989).

Figure 9 How the Lojack System Works

How one system works

In Massachusetts, the Lojack system is used in foiling automobile thieves. After the theft is reported, the police enter the vehicle's identification number into the state police data bank. The computer then sends a signal, using police radio towers, to the hidden receiver-transmitter in the stolen car.

Police Antenna

The signal causes the device to start broadcasting a code that can be picked up by police cruisers equipped with Lojack tracking computers in an area of 19 to 40 square km.

Stolen car

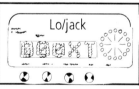

Tracking computer

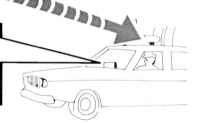

Lo/jack

When the stolen car comes within range of a cruiser with a computer, a device in the cruiser beeps and displays the location of the stolen car as well as a five-digit code. The police officer then types the code into the cruiser's computer and immediately receives a description of the stolen car, along with information about whether the theft occurred in conjunction with another crime. The police can then plan how to approach the vehicle.

Source: *The New York Times* 2 September 1989. Copyright © 1989 by The New York Times Company. Reprinted by permission.

Electronic engine immobilisation: New electronic engine management systems which disable a section of the system may provide an additional means of immobilising the engine, but the detailed design of the system will require development.

Case study: Australian immobilisation device

Recommended by police, insurance companies and the Royal Automobile Club of Victoria, a fail-proof immobilisation device was developed in 1985 by two Melbourne businessmen. The device retails for $395.

Two micro-switches which are hidden in the car and attached to hidden wiring under the bonnet, render useless the car's fuel system and electronics. Under supervised tests, professional car thieves took two days to steal a car fitted with the device.

Hire car companies are using the device, car salesmen are recommending it to buyers, and 200 police vehicles have been fitted with it. According to newspaper reports (*Melbourne Herald* 9 August 1989), not one of the 8,000 purchasers has reported their vehicle stolen.

Personal ignition entry code: The driver must enter a personal code using the trip computer: this code is interpreted by the engine management system and the engine can only be started if the code is correct.

Figure 10 *Personal Security Code Mechanism*

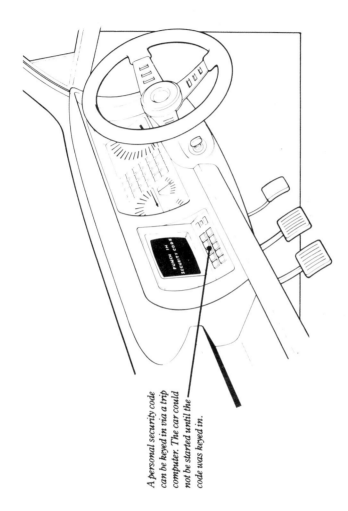

A personal security code can be keyed in via a trip computer. The car could not be started until the code was keyed in.

Source: United Kingdom Home Office 1985, *Design Solutions to Autocrime*. Reproduced with the permission of the Controller of Her Majesty's Stationery Office, London.

Key Code: In this device, the ignition key code — embodied in the profile of the conventional key, for example — is translated into an electronic code by the 'lock'. This code is then transmitted to the engine system where it is interpreted. Such systems will become feasible when multiplexing systems begin to appear on cars.

Human error: the unlocked car

As we noted previously, education campaigns exhorting motorists to lock up their cars, keep valuables out of sight, park off street, etc. enjoy limited success. An alternative is to design human fallibility out of the car as far as possible — to make the car more intelligent than the driver.

For example, people can be prevented from leaving their cars unlocked by central locking which operates when the key is removed from the ignition and the doors closed. Or cars can provide an audible warning to the driver. Cars on sale in the United States have a buzzer to remind the driver to remove the key from the ignition. British researchers costed this at about £2 ($4) as a standard feature. With some modification, and making use of, say, the courtesy light switches, this could be extended to remind drivers to lock doors.

Environmental design strategies

Controlling access

Thieves and vandals are more likely to hit targets which are easy to get in and out of, where a fast getaway is possible.

According to Poyner and Webb's United Kingdom studies (1987), controlling access to car parks can reduce car theft. Fewer cars will be stolen from large parking areas if entrances and exits are supervised by security personnel, they maintain. This supervision does not have to be particularly thorough: the presence of security guards or manned barriers appeared to reduce the incidence of car theft.

Electronic access control also seems to work. Poyner and Webb's analysis of autocrime statistics on the South Acton Housing Estate in West London revealed that hand-held devices activating roller doors, plus an increase in the number of parking bays available to tenants, cut autocrime by three-quarters between 1980 and 1986.

A combination of surveillance and environmental design modifications limiting access by pedestrians has also proven successful in reducing car theft, noticeably in the multi-storey, long-stay council car park in Dover, England (Poyner & Webb 1987).

Case study: preventing car theft in Dover

Environmental design modifications to a multi-storey, long-stay council car park in Dover, England, dramatically reduced car theft by restricting pedestrian access to the car park. Users who had abandoned the car park returned and revenue increased. The cost of the crime prevention program equalled one year's repair bills.

By 1983 Dover authorities realised that their security program, which combined private security officers patrolling the car park at night and random visits from council inspectors during the day, was not working. Vandalism was a problem — graffiti; broken windows; damage to lifts, doors, sand buckets and fire extinguishers; and defecation on stairs.

As part of the crime prevention program, gaps between the low walls around the ground floor of the car park were filled with wire mesh; the pedestrian entrance by the staircase was fitted with a self-closing steel door so that it could be used only as an exit; lighting at the main entrance and the pedestrian exit door was improved; and to provide surveillance, an office was built beside the main entrance and leased to a taxi firm operating 24 hours a day.

But while thefts *of* cars fell by 84 per cent in the multi-storey car park, thefts of items *from* cars was not affected by the improvements in security.

Poyner and Webb concluded that car thefts were committed by outsiders with no business in the car park, but thefts *from* cars were done either by legitimate users tempted by opportunity, or people who drove in specifically to steal. Environmental prevention measures worked against the car thieves, but were useless in dealing with determined petty thieves.

Case study: preventing car theft in a New York Port Authority car park

The New York Port Authority had a major problem with car theft in one of its parking lots. Juveniles would sneak into the lot at night, hot wire a car and drive it through the cyclone fence. Then other juveniles would drive cars away through the hole in the fence.

Erection of a concrete strip, about two feet high, around the outside of the cyclone fence prevented cars from being driven through. This measure reduced car theft from 179 cases in one year to zero the next (personal communication, from New York Port Authority to one of the authors).

Surveillance

Surveillance can take two forms — natural surveillance or organised surveillance.

Natural surveillance arises out of siting buildings — or in this case, car parks — so that passers-by, workers or nearby residents can easily monitor what is happening there. It generally requires good lighting and no obstructing walls, hedges or trees.

Formal organised surveillance can be professional security patrols, citizens' watch groups or electronic security such as closed circuit television (CCTV).

Case study: CCTV Surrey University car park

Surrey University, in the United Kingdom, had four main open car parks around its perimeter, all some distance from buildings and residences. Thefts from these car parks were the major crime problem on campus in 1984 and 1985.

Hedges bordering car parks and the perimeter road were trimmed to increase surveillance, lights were left on longer and £30,000 worth of closed circuit television was installed. Cameras were set high to minimise interference or vandalism and to maximise their range and sweep. They also had infrared vision for night-time surveillance and were connected to loudspeakers. As car park 4 was the focus of much of the autocrime on campus, one CCTV camera was positioned on top of a tower overlooking it and car park 3.

By greatly extending the ability of existing security staff to supervise large open parking areas, one CCTV camera and monitoring equipment reduced thefts from cars parked on campus by 66 per cent (Poyner & Webb 1987).

Case study: crime in Canberra car parks

In response to community concern about a spate of violent attacks on women in inner-Canberra early in 1988, the then Minister for the Australian Capital Territory issued instructions to improve surveillance in car parks in Civic by trimming hedges and shrubbery and improving lighting. Seven areas in the inner city were targeted for improvement, including three car parks and lanes leading from car parks to entertainment complexes.

Case study: combat auto theft

A program called Combat Automobile Theft, conceived in 1986 by a State Senator, started out in two precincts of Queens, New York, and has spread to 28 precincts city-wide.

Most of the cars stolen in the United States are stolen in the early morning. The program takes advantage of that fact. Car owners sign a consent form allowing police to stop their vehicle if it is being driven between 1 am and 5 am. Normally police are prohibited under the Fourth Amendment from stopping a car without cause, but the owner's statement creates a reasonable suspicion that a crime is in progress.

Yellow car stickers on the car windows warn thieves that the owner is in the program. The stickers have proven to be a remarkably effective deterrent. Of the 17,871 cars enrolled in the program, only 18 have been stolen in two years — a rate dramatically below the city average (*New York Times* 2 October 1988).

Cost

In its *Design Solutions to Autocrime* published in 1985, the United Kingdom Home Office maintained that, if an integrated security package design approach were adopted for mass-produced cars, significant and real increases in protection could be achieved at little, if any cost — certainly with a few tens of pounds. Even the application of the more sophisticated options need add less than 1 per cent to the cost of a car, they said.

Government initiatives

In 1987-88 119,966 motor vehicles valued at an estimated $599.83 million were stolen Australia-wide, compared to 132,675 worth $663.375 million in the previous financial year (*ICA Bulletin* February 1989).

In NSW, car thefts fell by over 12,000, the reduction being attributed by the Insurance Council of Australia partly to a car theft prevention campaign developed in 1988 by the State Intelligence Group of the New South Wales Police Force. The Group's 11-point strategy included surveillance of car parks, training programs about car theft for police, a feasibility study on a car theft phone-in reward scheme and a recommendation to the public to install anti-theft devices.

New registration regulations

An initiative taken by the New South Wales Government Department of Motor Transport (now the Roads and Traffic Authority) in October 1988 should discourage car thieves by making stolen cars impossible to register and therefore impossible to sell to unwary buyers. This scheme will work by requiring proof of identity from those transferring registration or registering cars for the first time, thus safeguarding innocent people from buying stolen cars.

For second-hand cars purchased interstate, new owners will have to supply evidence of previous registration or evidence of purchase if the car has been unregistered for some time. In addition, owners will have to supply a clearance from the vehicle encumbrance registers in other states to show that finance companies or banks are not the real owners.

As of January 1989, all new vehicles must be fitted with a standard format identification number. Vehicle manufacturers will have to notify the New South Wales Department of Motor Transport of the numbers before the Department will agree to register the vehicles in New South Wales. Any vehicle with a number not notified by its manufacturer will not be registered

By February 1989 the New South Wales Government was claiming that its tough new policies on car theft had resulted in a big drop in the number of cars stolen (*Sydney Morning Herald* 16 February 1989).

Increased penalties

By making car stealing a specific offence under the *Crimes Act*, the New South Wales government doubled the maximum jail sentence for car thieves to ten years as of February 1989. Joy-riding continues to attract a maximum five years in jail.

The *NSW Motor Traffic Act 1976* has also been amended to raise the penalty for illegal use of a vehicle from $500 to $2,000.

Component marking

Car theft for spare parts by professional gangs is a major problem in the United States, and was the subject of a report by a special task force to the Australian Police Ministers' Council in March 1989.

In 1984 the *Motor Vehicle Theft Law Enforcement Act* was passed in the United States, under which all major component parts on manufactured vehicles were to be numbered on models that exceeded a given theft rate. By law, manufacturers must now mark all the major sheet metal parts of many new cars with vehicle identification numbers (VINs) to allow stolen vehicles to be detected, particularly when those vehicles have been disassembled.

United States manufacturers had already been marking some car parts for some years; for example, the engine, transmission, frame and dashboard, and least two 'confidential' or hidden VINs.

Evidence on the effectiveness of component marking is equivocal. Following their pilot marking programs which involved only a few models, both General Motors and Ford concluded that parts marking did not appear greatly to affect auto theft. On the other hand, a program initiated by the State of Kentucky was highly successful: only three out of 60,000 marked vehicles were stolen. Evaluation of the national Car Rental System's marking program of its Chicago fleet revealed a decrease in car thefts from 27 cars in a one-year period to two cars in the next, and an increased recovery rate — up from 65 per cent to 92 per cent.

Clarke and Harris (1989) have evaluated the component marking provisions of the United States legislation and found them misconceived because only 'high-risk' models are involved, and the definition of high-risk is flawed.

A number of identification systems are available. The United States and Brazil use the 3M Confirm Automotive Labelling System, in which the label breaks up when removed and leaves a footprint visible under ultra violet light. These labels can be applied at the manufacturing stage or on used vehicles for a fee.

Ron Clarke believes an Australian component marking program would stand a reasonable chance of success if all new cars were marked, not only 'high-risk' cars and an even better chance if old cars were included. As a reason for including old cars, he cites the success of a West German initiative in the 1960s, in which all cars, old and new, were required by law to be fitted with steering locks — namely, a 60 per cent drop in car thefts.

Getting tough with juvenile offenders

The abolition of the juvenile cautioning system — in which juveniles were immune from prosecution for a first offence — and the introduction of a new law dealing specifically with car theft are credited by the authorities with a 7 per cent fall in car thefts in New South Wales in 1988. However, a proper evaluation is required before we can accept this fall as being due to abolition of the cautioning system. Police Department figures showed a 4,000 drop in the number of cars reported stolen in 1988, from 56,153 down to 52,240. According to these statistics, the most dramatic fall was in the last quarter of 1988, when fewer than 123,000 cars were stolen, the lowest quarterly figure since March 1982 (New South Wales Police Department 1988).

Theft from cars

Improved surveillance has proven effective in reducing theft from cars in open car parks. At Surrey University in the United Kingdom, the use of closed circuit television by security staff reduced thefts (for details, see Case study, p.38); and on the Pepys housing estate in London, increased police surveillance during a major crack-down on drug dealing dramatically reduced thefts from vehicles on and around the estate (Poyner & Webb 1987).

Check list

The most obvious solution to much theft from cars is common-sense prevention, for example:

- Make sure your car is locked.
- Never leave keys in the ignition.
- Park your car where you can see it.
- Do not leave valuables in your car.
- If you must leave possessions in your car, hide them from sight.

Public housing car parks: special problems

Car parks can be the source of many problems on public housing estates — not only car theft and theft from cars, but also vandalism and danger to residents from intruders, especially at night.

Some crime prevention strategies follow.

Theft and vandalism

- Wherever possible, provide each dwelling with its own locked garage within the property boundaries. Locked garages outside the boundaries or well-lit and visible common car parks are the next best thing.

- Where private garages are not feasible, a car-port or driveway parking is preferable to grouped parking away from dwellings.

- As a general rule, underground or multi-storey car parks should be avoided, as they are breeding grounds for vandalism and crime. If they already exist, danger could be minimised by limiting entry points and providing these with sturdy locked gates. Alternatively, each resident could be provided with a lockable garage in their own space, with robust, vandalproof metal doors — garages within garages, so to speak. Or users can be provided with a secure lock or a plastic keycard which operates electronic doors.

- Grouped car parks should be avoided in high-crime areas. If they cannot be avoided, they should be within view of some dwellings; they should be equipped with sturdy gates or tiltadoors, and should never be sited near alleyways.

• Open car parks should be small and within view of dwellings and visitors' car parks should be clearly identifiable, well lit, and visible from dwellings.

Rape, assault, robbery

• To make car parks safer, planners should provide direct access from parking areas to the entrance of dwellings.

• Car parks should be no further than 60 metres from dwellings, and the path should be well lit and free from shrubbery.

• Visitors' car parks should be well lit, clearly identifiable, and visible from dwellings.

• Access to enclosed car parks should be limited to residents by some form of electronic entry control device if possible.

• If it is desirable to limit access to dwellings, make sure access via car parks is monitored as well.

• In high-crime areas, advanced technological surveillance methods may be needed in car parks. For example, an infrared unit is available which detects the presence of intruders — but not cats and dogs — by body heat, and automatically switches on all lights in the car park and turns them off after 15 to 20 minutes.

Bibliography

Austin Rover News 6 December 1988, "The Rover Security Concepts Car", Austin Rover Group Limited External Affairs, Coventry, England.

Burney, John February 1988, "It's so easy", *The Open Road*, NRMA, Sydney.

Clarke, R.V.G 1987, "Crime Prevention — Car Theft Strategies", in *Car Theft. Putting on the Brakes*, Proceedings of a seminar organised by the NRMA in association with the Australian Institute of Criminology, 21 May.

Clarke, R.V.G. & Harris, Patti 1989, unpublished paper evaluating the *Motor Vehicle Theft Law Prevention Act 1984.*

Daily Mail (London) 7 December 1988, "The car the 'experts' couldn't steal".

Geason, Susan & Wilson, Paul R. 1988, *Crime prevention: theory and practice*, Australian Institute of Criminology, Canberra.

ICA Bulletin February 1989, "Car Theft...There are no exceptions!" Insurance Council of Australia.

Mayhew, Patricia, Clarke, R.V.G., Sturman, A. & Hough, J.M. 1976, *Crime as Opportunity*, HMSO, London.

Melbourne Herald 7 August 1989, "Car thefts reach $30 million".

Melbourne Herald 8 August 1989, "In 30 seconds, your car is his".

New South Wales Police Department 1988, *NSW Crime Statistics 1987-88 Financial Year*, Annex to 1987-88 Annual Report.

NRMA 16 February 1989, "Car thefts fall by nearly 4,000".

NRMA Insurance Ltd. May 1987, *Car Theft in NSW. A Special Report*, Sydney.

NRMA 1987, *Car Theft: Putting on the Brakes*. Proceedings of a seminar organised by the NRMA in association with the Australian Institute of Criminology, Sydney.

NRMA May 1988, *Car Theft in New South Wales. An Update*, Sydney.

NRMA May 1989, *Car Theft in New South Wales. An Update*, Sydney.

New York Times 30 September 1988, "Antidote for Auto Theft".

New York Times 2 September 1989, "Follow This Car! I'm Being Stolen".

Organised Motor Vehicle Theft Task Force March 1989, *Report to Australian Police Ministers' Council.*

Poyner, Barry & Webb, Barry 1987, *Successful Crime Prevention. Case Studies*, The Tavistock Institute of Human Relations, London.

Southall, Dean & Ekblom, Paul 1985, *Designing for Vehicle Security: towards a crime free car*, Crime Prevention Unit Paper 4, UK Home Office, London.

Sun Herald 19 February 1989, "10 Years for Car Thieves".

Sunday Times (London) October 9 1988, "Debut of the theft-proof car".

Sydney Morning Herald 3 June 1988, "Car thieves put Sydney on the map".

Sydney Morning Herald 16 February 1989, "Car thefts fall by nearly 4,000".

Sydney Morning Herald 9 May 1989, "Great car-theft racket: one goes every 10 minutes".

Sydney Morning Herald 9 May 1989, "Police in $1b stolen car racket".

United Kingdom Home Office 1985, *Design Solutions to Autocrime*, HMSO, London.

Weekend Australian 3-4 December 1988, "GM-H banks on magic box deadlocks to foil car thieves".